Single Sweets

Delicious, Allergen-Free Desserts for One

Created, Designed, and Photographed by

KRISTIN OSIKA

Table of Contents

"All our dreams can come true, if we have the courage to pursue them"
- Walt Disney

Introduction

Growing up with celiac disease, the phrase "No thank you, I'm gluten free" became an essential part of my vocabulary. At social gatherings, school, or when visiting family, I frequently needed to bring my own desserts and watch as others enjoyed delicious treats I could not eat.

Most people with allergies or dietary restrictions have experienced similar circumstances, and sometimes, eating an processed, allergen-free cookie just doesn't beat watching others enjoy a homemade lava cake. Yet, this seems to be the reality: allergen-free desserts are often difficult to make at home, and typically, they are not as satisfying as "regular" baked goods.

With one ramekin, ten minutes, and a passion for baking, I set out to prove these notions false. As someone who has always needed to bring a "special" dessert to events, I realized the idea of a specific, allergen-friendly dessert for one could be reshaped in an entirely new (and positive) light. I imagined a reality in which eating that "special" dessert could make someone happier than eating a generic treat alongside everyone else.

Just like that, single sweets were born. Personalized to taste, specific to dietary need, and *incredibly* easy to make, single sweets provide a safe, individualized alternative to dessert-deficient sadness.

So, what are single sweets? Let's start with the basics:

- Every recipe is free of the top eight allergens, or it can be easily (and effectively) modified to exclude them. Anyone avoiding...

wheat, milk, eggs, peanuts, tree nuts, soy, fish, or shellfish

  ...can find many single sweets to suit their needs. Vegan, paleo, refined sugar-free, and grain-free options are also included.

- There is no need to preheat the oven or start the stove; every single sweet can be made in the microwave. You'll need a ramekin (see page seven), something to mix with (such as a spoon, fork, or whisk), and maybe an extra small bowl (only as needed for a few recipes).

- Using just a few, well-known ingredients, *Single Sweets* advocates easy, simple baking. You won't see any obscure, hard-to-find ingredients, or complicated cooking tactics. With a tablespoon of this, a pinch of that, and several seconds in the microwave, your dessert is ready. That's it!

Why Single Sweets?

Single sweets take less than eight minutes to make and less than two minutes to bake.

The top eight allergens (all of which can be excluded from single sweets) are responsible for 90% of all food allergies in the United States. The remaining 10% of allergies are largely specific to ingredients not commonly found in desserts, which means everyone can find a single sweet to safely enjoy.

Single sweets are perfect for families in which every member has different tastes or allergies, causing them to enjoy different treats; however, single sweets aren't only for those with dietary restrictions. Everyone can enjoy them! Best of all, those without allergies will never realize their dessert is any different from a "regular" one you might find in a bakery. With flavors from lemon blueberry to ginger molasses to chocolate cherry, even the pickiest of eaters can find a single sweet they adore.

I have created 35 recipes to make your friends and family jealous of *your* dessert - not the other way around. Before you know it, you'll be excited about dessert again!

XOXO,

Kristin

Ingredients & Supplies

Flour

Today, it is easy and convenient to find allergen-free flour blends on store shelves. Hauling home ten different flours to divide, measure, and combine is no longer necessary to create delicious, allergen-free desserts. Nevertheless, flours come in numerous varieties and blend combinations, and it can be confusing and difficult to decide which is best to use.

When a *Single Sweets* recipe calls for gluten-free flour, I recommend using an all-purpose, 1:1 flour blend which includes a thickener (such as xanthan gum) and a base of brown rice flour and potato starch. I have found this combination produces the best results, and for the most part, it is not gummy or sticky. My blend of choice is King Arthur's gluten-free 1:1 flour. Of course, be sure to check that the flour you use is free of any allergens you avoid.

An all-purpose flour blend with wheat could be substituted 1:1 for gluten-free flour in any recipe if desired, though **recipes are optimized for use with the ingredients listed**. Note that no substitution can be made for coconut flour.

Fat

Oil and butter are the most commonly used fats in baking. In most *Single Sweets* recipes, oil is needed, and any neutral oil can be used, including vegetable, avocado, canola, or liquid coconut oil. *Single Sweets* recipes which call for butter do benefit greatly from its rich flavor; unsalted butter from a stick works best. For a vegan or dairy-free option, my go-to is the avocado oil spread by Pure Blends. Any plant-based spread will have a similar effect as butter, if it has a high fat content and neutral taste.

Milk

In recent years, replacing cow's milk in baking has become easier and easier. In addition to traditional milk, a variety of delicious plant-based and alternative milks are now available, including almond, coconut, oat, soy, rice, and hemp milk.

When a *Single Sweets* recipe calls for nondairy milk, I recommend using plain, unsweetened coconut milk from a carton due to its rich flavor and low fat content. Oat milk is another fantastic alternative. Other low-fat milks will work in any given recipe, but if you choose to use high-fat milks, the dessert may need a longer baking time. Make sure the milk you choose is unsweetened, or your dessert might end up being too sweet.

On the lookout

Reading ingredients and the fine print on food labels can certainly be tedious, but it is absolutely necessary for anyone avoiding one or many common allergens. Some foods need special attention before buying, as frequently they can be cross-contaminated or even contain a discrete allergen.

Food labels commonly display statements such as:

"Processed in a facility that also processes _____"
"May Contain _____ "
"Contains _____"

Every one of these phrases should put someone with allergies on high alert: it is safest to avoid foods with any of these statements pertaining to an ingredient you are allergic to.

Below are some ingredients to always double check before including in Single Sweets:

Chocolate - Generic chocolate chips almost always contain dairy, and they are frequently cross-contaminated with nuts, soy, wheat, and gluten. I opt for Enjoy Life chocolate chips and chocolate bars, as they are free of the top eight food allergens.

Oats - Oats can be tricky. At first glance, they might seem to be allergen-friendly; however, oats are frequently cross-contaminated with wheat and gluten. Make sure to use oats labelled gluten-free when you bake!

Additionally, always be wary of **graham crackers, cookies, chips, pretzels, granola, and cereals**.

It is easy to forget to check an ingredient's label before including that ingredient in a recipe. Don't worry! Below every recipe which contains one of the ingredients above, you will find a note reminding you to check the label before using the ingredient.

A Word of Caution: *Coconut*
Coconut is a seed from a drupe (a type of fruit), and few people allergic to tree nuts have any reaction to coconut; however, in the fall of 2006, the Food and Drug Administration (FDA) decided that coconut would be considered a tree nut for food labelling purposes.

Despite the FDA's decision, according to Food Allergy Research and Education (FARE), the people who are allergic to coconut almost always do not have coinciding or correlated allergies to tree nuts. As a result, coconut is included in numerous *Single Sweets* recipes, and it is recommended as the optimal type of nondairy milk to use when baking. If you do avoid coconut, I would recommend substituting oat milk for coconut milk and avoiding recipes which contain shredded coconut.

It is recommended that you always err on the side of caution, and **check with your doctor or allergist before consuming coconut** if you have other allergies to nuts.

Ramekins

Ramekins are ceramic bowls designed to fit small desserts. They are completely heat-resistant, and they are both microwave- and oven-safe. Since ramekins are not as large or deep as a mug, baking in them takes a minimal amount of time, and you will not need a long spoon to reach the bottom for the last crumbs of a dessert.

In every *Single Sweets* recipe, it is best to use a four-ounce ramekin: this is the perfect size for any dessert for one. Cakes rise perfectly to the top of the ramekin, while shorter desserts (such as cookies) are easy to reach and eat due to the ramekin's shallow height.

If you don't have a ramekin on hand, I would recommend using a four-ounce glass bowl instead. If you choose to use a bowl or mug larger than four ounces in capacity, it may take longer to cook your single sweet; cooking in a paper cup, on the other hand, may take less time. Whatever dish you choose, be sure to check it is microwave-safe before baking your dessert in it.

Some recipes might require an additional bowl for mixing or melting ingredients. My same suggestions apply here: it is best to use a four-ounce ramekin or glass bowl.

Microwaves

A microwave provides a quick, easy, and effective way to reheat and cook a variety of foods. It seems almost magical: if you place a dish inside and press a few buttons, in just several seconds, any food can be transformed. From reheating meals to baking desserts, microwaves are versatile and can be used for a variety of culinary purposes.

How exactly do microwaves work?
Microwaves direct a specific type of electromagnetic (EM) waves towards a dish. These EM waves cause water molecules in the food to vibrate and quickly heat up, warming the food without heating the inside of the microwave as well.

Whereas temperatures inside of an oven can reach higher than 400° F, any cookware or food placed inside of a microwave rarely warms to higher than 212° F. This temperature difference can have a few implications in baking: for example, cakes will not develop a golden crust on their exterior. Nevertheless, a microwave uses significantly less energy than an oven, and desserts baked in the microwave still taste fantastic. Best of all, microwave baking is **extremely efficient**: desserts which might typically take up to an hour to bake in a regular oven can be baked in a microwave in just minutes.

KNOW YOUR MICROWAVE.

I cannot stress these three words enough. Microwaves vary drastically by brand, age, model, and many other factors. Some might cook food quickly, slowly, or unevenly, and as a result, timing can be quite tricky.

Every single sweet has been tested and developed for an **900 watt microwave**. If your microwave has a wattage higher than 900, I would recommend reducing the baking time by five to ten seconds. For those with a lower-wattage microwave, you may need to add five to ten seconds extra.

Single sweets continue to bake for the first few minutes after they are removed from the microwave (even more so if they are covered). For this reason, when you remove your dessert from the microwave, I would recommend leaving it slightly underbaked rather than adding extra time and overbaking, if you must choose. Since all single sweets are egg-free, there isn't much to worry about if you consume raw dough or batter. Nothing beats an ooey-gooey, melts-in-your-mouth dessert, especially not one which has been cooked for too long and is gummy.

Measurement Conversions

Reference this table to convert measurements with ease.
Numbers are rounded to the closest equivalent.

Ounces	Cups	Tablespoons	Teaspoons	Volumes
4 oz	½ cup	8 tablespoons	24 teaspoons	118 mL
3 oz	⅜ cup	6 tablespoons	18 teaspoons	90 mL
2.5 oz	⅓ cup	5 ⅓ tablespoons	16 teaspoons	79 mL
2 oz	¼ cup	4 tablespoons	12 teaspoons	59 mL
1 oz	⅛ cup	2 tablespoons	6 teaspoons	30 mL
½ oz	⅟₁₆ cup	1 tablespoon	3 teaspoons	15 mL
			1 teaspoon	5 mL
			½ teaspoon	2 ½ mL
			¼ teaspoon	1 ¼ mL
			⅛ teaspoon	A dash
			⅟₁₆ teaspoon	A pinch or drop

Lifestyle-Friendly Recipes

No matter your dietary needs or preferences, there is a single sweet for you.

Paleo

Honey Chia Pudding
Coconut Macaroon

Refined Sugar-Free

Honey Chia Pudding
Coconut Macaroon
Frosted Maple Cake

Grain-Free

Honey Chia Pudding
Coconut Macaroon
Crustless Pumpkin Pie

Vegan

Berries and Jam Layer Cake
Chocolate Dream Cake
Coffee Cake
Pineapple Upside Down Cake
Zucchini Bread
Orange Cranberry Bread
Caramelized Banana Bread
Blackberry Plum Cake
Coconut Lime Pudding
Crustless Pumpkin Pie
Blueberry Crumble
Apple Cinnamon Crisp
Ginger Pear Crisp
Oatmeal Raisin Cookie
Ginger Molasses Cookie

VEGAN, with adjustments:

Vanilla Sprinkles Cake
(with vegan sprinkles)
Carrot Cake
(with vegan cream cheese in the frosting)
Chocolate Mint Lava Cake
(with vegan chocolate)
Frosted Maple Cake
(with vegan butter in the frosting)

VEGAN with adjustments:
continued

Raspberry Brown Sugar Cake
(with vegan butter)
Black Forest Torte
(with vegan chocolate)
Chocolate Cloud Pudding
(with vegan chocolate)
Glazed Peach Pie
(with vegan butter)
Mango Matcha Tart
(with vegan butter)
Chocolate Chip Cookie
(with vegan chocolate)
Double Chocolate Coffee Cookie
(with vegan chocolate)
Spoonable Cookie Dough
(with vegan chocolate)
Lemon Shortbread Cookie
(with vegan butter)
Dark Chocolate Brownie
(with vegan chocolate)

Be sure to always check individual labels to
confirm that all the ingredients used are vegan.

Cakes & Breads

Berries & Jam Layer Cake

INGREDIENTS

Berry Filling:
2 tablespoons mixed berries
1 teaspoon sugar
½ teaspoon cornstarch

Cake:
2 tablespoons gluten-free flour
2 teaspoons sugar
¼ teaspoon baking powder
Pinch of salt
2 tablespoons nondairy milk
½ teaspoon oil
⅛ teaspoon vanilla extract

DIRECTIONS

To make the filling:
Microwave the mixed berries in a small bowl for 30 seconds (900 watts), or until soft.
Add the sugar and cornstarch, and microwave for an additional 20 seconds (900 watts). The mixture will have the consistency of a thick jam.

To make the cake:
In another small bowl, combine the flour, sugar, baking powder, and salt.
Mix in the milk, oil, and vanilla extract.

IN A RAMEKIN, alternate pouring the batter and spreading the jam until you fill up the dish. Microwave for one minute (900 watts). Let cool for two minutes, then enjoy!

*NOTES
Use a toothpick to spread the jam into the flower shape pictured.

Vanilla Sprinkles Cake

INGREDIENTS

3 tablespoons gluten-free flour
1 tablespoon + 1 teaspoon sugar
¼ teaspoon baking powder
Pinch of salt
2 tablespoons nondairy milk
1 teaspoon oil
¼ teaspoon vanilla extract
Sprinkles, to taste

DIRECTIONS

IN A RAMEKIN, combine the flour, sugar, baking powder, and salt.
Mix in the milk, oil, and vanilla extract.
Stir in the sprinkles.
Microwave for one minute (900 watts).
Let cool for two minutes.
Enjoy!

Chocolate Dream Cake

INGREDIENTS

2 tablespoons gluten-free flour
1 tablespoon unsweetened
 cocoa powder
1 tablespoon sugar
¼ teaspoon baking powder
Pinch of instant coffee powder*
Pinch of salt
2 tablespoons nondairy milk
2 teaspoons oil

DIRECTIONS

IN A RAMEKIN, combine the flour, cocoa powder, sugar, baking powder, coffee powder, and salt.
Add in the milk and oil, and mix to combine.
Microwave for one minute (900 watts).
Let cool for two minutes.
Top with powdered sugar, if desired.
Enjoy!

*NOTES
The addition of instant coffee powder makes the chocolate flavor big, bold, and delicious, and you won't taste any coffee flavor at all.

Honey Swirl Cake

INGREDIENTS

1 ½ tablespoons nondairy milk
1 tablespoon honey
2 teaspoons oil
¼ teaspoon vanilla extract
3 tablespoons gluten-free flour
1 tablespoon sugar
¼ teaspoon baking powder
Pinch of salt
Honey, to taste

DIRECTIONS

IN A RAMEKIN, mix together the milk, honey, oil, and vanilla extract.
Add the flour, sugar, baking powder, and salt, and stir until the ingredients are fully combined.
Microwave for one minute (900 watts).
Let the cake cool for two minutes.
Drizzle extra honey in a swirl on top of the cake, then enjoy!

Coffee Cake

INGREDIENTS

Cake:
3 tablespoons gluten-free flour
¼ teaspoon baking powder
¼ teaspoon cinnamon
2 ½ tablespoons nondairy milk
1 ½ tablespoons brown sugar
½ tablespoon oil

Topping:
2 teaspoons brown sugar
¼ teaspoon cinnamon

DIRECTIONS

To make the cake:
IN A RAMEKIN, whisk together the flour, baking powder, and cinnamon.
Add the milk, brown sugar, and oil, and mix until the batter is smooth.

To make the topping:
In a small bowl, mix the brown sugar and cinnamon. Then, sprinkle the topping over the cake batter.

Microwave for one minute (900 watts).
Let cool for two minutes, then enjoy!

Carrot Cake

INGREDIENTS

3 tablespoons gluten-free flour
1 tablespoon sugar
¼ teaspoon baking powder
⅛ teaspoon cinnamon
Pinch of nutmeg
Pinch of allspice
Pinch of salt
2 tablespoons shredded carrots
2 tablespoons nondairy milk
2 teaspoons oil

DIRECTIONS

IN A RAMEKIN, combine the flour, sugar, baking powder, cinnamon, nutmeg, allspice, and salt.
Mix in the carrots, milk, and oil.
Microwave for one minute (900 watts).
Let cool for two minutes.
For the best flavor, chill the cake in the refrigerator for at least an hour.
Top with the cream cheese frosting.
Enjoy!

Cream Cheese Frosting

In a small bowl, whisk together
2 tablespoons room temperature cream cheese (substitude vegan cream cheese as needed) **with**
1 teaspoon nondairy milk and
1 tablespoon powdered sugar.
Enjoy!

Chocolate Mint Lava Cake

INGREDIENTS

3 tablespoons chocolate chips*
½ teaspoon oil
⅛ teaspoon peppermint extract
1 tablespoon nondairy milk
2 tablespoons gluten-free flour
1 teaspoon sugar
¼ teaspoon baking powder
½ ounce semisweet baking
  chocolate, chopped*
2 teaspoons water

DIRECTIONS

IN A RAMEKIN, combine the chocolate chips, oil, and peppermint extract.
Microwave for 45 seconds (900 watts). Stir in the milk, and microwave for an additional 15 seconds (900 watts).
Add the flour, sugar, and baking powder, and mix until smooth.
Place the baking chocolate in the center of the batter, and press down slightly.
Pour the water over the chocolate, but do not mix. Leave the layer of water on top of the cake.
Microwave for 45 seconds (900 watts).
Let cool for two minutes, then enjoy!

*NOTES
Always check the ingredient label of the chocolate chips and baking chocolate to ensure they are free of any allergens you avoid (see page six).
½ ounce of chopped baking chocolate is about 1 tablespoon.

Pineapple Upside Down Cake

INGREDIENTS

Pineapple Layer:
1 tablespoon crushed pineapple*
1 teaspoon brown sugar
½ teaspoon oil

Cake:
2 tablespoons gluten-free flour
½ tablespoon unsweetened
    shredded coconut
¼ teaspoon baking powder
Pinch of salt
2 tablespoons crushed pineapple
1 tablespoon nondairy milk
½ tablespoon brown sugar
1 teaspoon oil
⅛ teaspoon vanilla extract

*NOTES
If you use canned crushed pineapple, make sure to drain any excess liquid before measuring.

DIRECTIONS

To make the pineapple layer:
IN A RAMEKIN, mix the crushed pineapple, brown sugar, and oil. Spread the mixture evenly over the bottom of the ramekin, and microwave for 15 seconds (900 watts).

To make the cake:
In another small bowl, mix the flour, coconut, baking powder, and salt.
Add the crushed pineapple, milk, brown sugar, oil, and vanilla extract, and stir until the batter is smooth. Pour the batter over the pineapple in the ramekin.
Microwave for one minute (900 watts). Let cool for two minutes.
Flip the cake out of the ramekin, then enjoy!

Frosted Maple Cake

INGREDIENTS

3 tablespoons gluten-free flour
¼ teaspoon baking powder
Pinch of salt
1 tablespoon + 1 teaspoon maple syrup
1 tablespoon nondairy milk
1 teaspoon oil
¼ teaspoon maple extract

Maple Frosting

In a small bowl, mix together
2 tablespoons butter (substitute a vegan buttery spread as needed), **2 tablespoons maple syrup**, and **⅛ teaspoon maple extract.** Enjoy!

DIRECTIONS

IN A RAMEKIN, mix the flour, baking powder, and salt. Add in the maple syrup, milk, oil, and maple extract, and stir until fully combined.
Microwave for one minute (900 watts).
Let cool for two minutes, then top with the maple frosting. Add maple sugar, if desired. Enjoy!

Raspberry Brown Sugar Cake

INGREDIENTS

1 ½ tablespoons butter (substitute a
 vegan buttery spread as needed)
2 tablespoons brown sugar
1 teaspoon nondairy milk
¼ teaspoon vanilla extract
3 tablespoons gluten-free flour
¼ teaspoon baking powder
Pinch of salt
1 tablespoon chopped fresh raspberries

DIRECTIONS

IN A RAMEKIN, microwave the butter for
15 seconds (900 watts), or until melted.
Stir in the brown sugar, then add the milk
and vanilla extract.
Mix in the flour, baking powder, and salt,
and stir until fully combined.
Fold in the raspberries.
Microwave for one minute (900 watts).
Let cool for two minutes. Top with brown
sugar, if desired, then enjoy!

Black Forest Torte

INGREDIENTS

Cherry Layer:
¼ cup chopped cherries
1 tablespoon mini chocolate chips*

Cake:
1 tablespoon gluten-free flour
½ tablespoon sugar
1 teaspoon unsweetened cocoa powder
⅛ teaspoon baking powder
Pinch of salt
1 ½ tablespoons nondairy milk
1 teaspoon oil

*NOTES
The batter will be thin.
Always check the ingredient label of
the chocolate chips to ensure they
are free of any allergens you avoid
(see page six).

DIRECTIONS

IN A RAMEKIN, mix the cherries and small
chocolate chips.

In a separate bowl, whisk together the flour,
sugar, cocoa powder, baking powder, and salt.
Stir in the milk and oil.*
Pour the chocolate batter over the cherries
and chocolate chips.
Microwave for one minute (900 watts).
Let cool for two minutes, and top with extra
cherries and chocolate chips, if desired.
Enjoy!

Zucchini Bread

INGREDIENTS

3 tablespoons gluten-free flour
¼ teaspoon baking powder
⅛ teaspoon cinnamon
Pinch of salt
3 tablespoons grated zucchini
1 ½ tablespoons brown sugar
2 teaspoons nondairy milk
1 teaspoon oil
⅛ teaspoon vanilla extract
1 tablespoon raisins

DIRECTIONS

IN A RAMEKIN, mix the flour, baking powder, cinnamon, and salt.
Add the zucchini, brown sugar, milk, oil, and vanilla extract, and mix until fully combined.
Stir in the raisins.
Microwave for one minute (900 watts).
Let cool for two minutes, then enjoy!

Orange Cranberry Bread

INGREDIENTS

3 tablespoons gluten-free flour
1 tablespoon sugar
¼ teaspoon baking powder
Pinch of salt
1 ½ tablespoons orange juice
1 teaspoon oil
¼ teaspoon orange zest
⅛ teaspoon vanilla extract
1 tablespoon chopped fresh cranberries

DIRECTIONS

IN A RAMEKIN, mix the flour, sugar, baking powder, and salt.
Add the orange juice, oil, orange zest, and vanilla extract, and mix until fully combined.
Fold in the cranberries.
Microwave for one minute (900 watts). Let cool for two minutes, then enjoy!

Caramelized Banana Bread

INGREDIENTS

Caramelized Banana Layer:
1 teaspoon brown sugar
½ teaspoon oil
5 banana slices

Bread:
2 tablespoons mashed, overripe banana
1 tablespoon nondairy milk
1 tablespoon brown sugar
1 teaspoon oil
¼ teaspoon vanilla extract
2 tablespoons gluten-free flour
¼ teaspoon baking powder
⅛ teaspoon cinnamon
Pinch of salt

DIRECTIONS

To make the caramelized bananas:
IN A RAMEKIN, mix the brown sugar and oil. Spread the mixture evenly over the bottom of the ramekin; lay the banana slices on top. Microwave for 15 seconds (900 watts).

To make the bread:
In another small bowl, mix the mashed banana, milk, brown sugar, oil, and vanilla extract.
Add in the flour, baking powder, cinnamon, and salt, and stir until smooth.
Pour the batter over the bananas in the ramekin.
Microwave for one minute (900 watts).
Let cool for two minutes.
Flip the cake out of the ramekin, then enjoy!

Blackberry Plum Cake

INGREDIENTS

Blackberry Plum Layer:
⅓ cup chopped blackberries and plums
1 teaspoon sugar
1 teaspoon cornstarch

Cake:
2 tablespoons gluten-free flour
1 tablespoon sugar
¼ teaspoon baking powder
Pinch of salt
2 tablespoons nondairy milk
1 teaspoon oil
Drop of vanilla extract

DIRECTIONS

IN A RAMEKIN, toss the blackberries and plums in the sugar and cornstarch.

In another small bowl, combine the flour, sugar, baking powder, and salt with the milk, oil, and vanilla extract.
Spoon the cake batter over the fruit in the ramekin. Using the back of a spoon, spread the batter so it forms an even layer.

Microwave for one minute (900 watts).
Cover the cake with a lid and let cool for five minutes. Enjoy!

Puddings, Pies, & Crisps

Coconut Lime Pudding

INGREDIENTS

¼ cup coconut milk*
1½ tablespoons sugar
1 tablespoon cornstarch
Pinch of salt
1 teaspoon lime juice

DIRECTIONS

IN A RAMEKIN, combine the coconut milk, sugar, cornstarch, and salt. Whisk **vigorously** until the mixture is **completely smooth**. Microwave for one minute (900 watts). Immediately stir in the lime juice, mixing continuously for at least 30 seconds. Serve immediately, or chill until you are ready to enjoy.* Top with lime zest, if desired.

*NOTES
Unsweetened coconut milk from a carton works best.
To prevent a skin from forming on top of the pudding, press plastic wrap directly on the surface of the pudding, then refrigerate.

Chocolate Cloud Pudding

INGREDIENTS

2 ½ tablespoons sugar
2 teaspoons cornstarch
1 teaspoon unsweetened cocoa powder
Pinch of salt
3 tablespoons + 2 tablespoons nondairy
  milk (separated)
¼ teaspoon vanilla extract
1 tablespoon chocolate chips*

DIRECTIONS

IN A RAMEKIN, combine the sugar, cornstarch, cocoa powder, salt, and 3 tablespoons milk. Microwave for 50 seconds (900 watts). Immediately mix in the 2 tablespoons milk, vanilla extract, and chocolate chips. Continue to stir until the chocolate chips are completely melted and the pudding has thickened.
Serve immediately, or chill until you are ready to enjoy.*

*NOTES
Always check the ingredient label of the chocolate chips to ensure they are free of any allergens you avoid (see page six).
To prevent a skin from forming on top of the pudding, press plastic wrap directly on the surface of the pudding, then refrigerate.

Honey Chia Pudding

INGREDIENTS

Pudding:
½ cup nondairy milk
½ tablespoon honey
2 tablespoons chia seeds

Toppings:
Honey
Berries
Banana
Cacao Nibs*

*NOTES
Always check the ingredient label of the
cacao nibs to ensure they are free of any
allergens you avoid (see page six).

DIRECTIONS

IN A RAMEKIN, mix the milk and honey.
Stir in the chia seeds, and refrigerate for at
least two hours, or overnight.
Top with honey, blueberries, bananas, and
cacao nibs, if you so choose. Enjoy!

Crustless Pumpkin Pie

INGREDIENTS

⅓ cup pumpkin puree*
1 tablespoon brown sugar
1 teaspoon nondairy milk
⅛ teaspoon pumpkin pie spice
⅛ teaspoon cinnamon
Pinch of salt

DIRECTIONS

IN A RAMEKIN, stir together all the ingredients. Mix until the filling is smooth and uniform. Microwave for two minutes (900 watts). Let cool for five minutes. Top with vegan whipped cream if desired, then enjoy!

*NOTES

Make sure to use pumpkin puree and not pumpkin pie filling. Pumpkin pie filling is already spiced and sweetened, so if included, it might change the pie's flavor dramatically.

Blueberry Crumble

INGREDIENTS

⅓ cup fresh blueberries
1 teaspoon sugar
½ teaspoon cornstarch
½ teaspoon lemon juice
1 tablespoon gluten-free
  old fashioned oats*
1 teaspoon gluten-free flour
1 teaspoon brown sugar
¼ teaspoon cinnamon
1 teaspoon oil

DIRECTIONS

IN A RAMEKIN, toss the blueberries with the sugar, cornstarch, and lemon juice. Set aside.

In another microwave-safe bowl, mix together the oats, flour, brown sugar, and cinnamon to create the oat crumble. Stir in the oil. Microwave the oat crumble for 30 seconds (900 watts). Mix well, then microwave for an additional 30 seconds (900 watts).

Sprinkle the topping over the blueberries in the ramekin, then microwave for 30 seconds (900 watts). Let cool for two minutes, then enjoy!

*NOTES
*Always check the ingredient label of the oats to ensure they are free of any allergens you avoid (see page six).

Apple Cinnamon Crisp

INGREDIENTS

Apple Cinnamon Filling:
⅓ cup chopped apples (about half of a medium apple)
1 teaspoon brown sugar
½ teaspoon cornstarch
⅛ teaspoon apple pie spice
⅛ teaspoon cinnamon

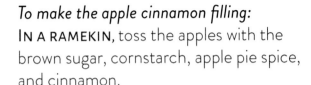

Topping:
1 tablespoon gluten-free old fashioned oats*
1 teaspoon gluten-free flour
1 teaspoon brown sugar
⅛ teaspoon cinnamon
Pinch of salt
1 teaspoon oil

*NOTES
*Always check the ingredient label of the oats to ensure they are free of any allergens you avoid (see page six).

DIRECTIONS

To make the apple cinnamon filling:
IN A RAMEKIN, toss the apples with the brown sugar, cornstarch, apple pie spice, and cinnamon.

To make the topping:
In another microwave-safe bowl, combine the oats, flour, brown sugar, cinnamon, and salt. Stir in the oil.

Microwave the topping for 30 seconds (900 watts). Mix well, then microwave for an additional 30 seconds (900 watts).

Sprinkle the topping over the apples, and microwave for one minute (900 watts). Let cool for two minutes, then enjoy!

Glazed Peach Pie

INGREDIENTS

1 tablespoon gluten-free flour
¼ teaspoon sugar
Dash of salt
½ tablespoon butter, room temperature
   (substitute a vegan buttery spread as
   needed)
⅓ cup sliced peaches

DIRECTIONS

IN A RAMEKIN, combine the flour, sugar, and salt. Mash in the butter with a fork, until the mixture is crumbly.

Flatten the dough into the bottom of the ramekin using the back of a spoon.

Microwave for 15 seconds (900 watts).

Arrange the peaches on top of the crust in the ramekin, and microwave for an additional 45 seconds (900 watts).

Let cool for two minutes. Top with the glaze, and enjoy!

Classic Glaze

In a small bowl, whisk together **1 tablespoon powdered sugar,** **½ teaspoon nondairy milk,** and a **drop of vanilla extract.** Drizzle or pour over the pie, as desired. Enjoy!

Ginger Pear Crisp

INGREDIENTS

Ginger Pear Filling:
½ cup chopped pears (about one small pear)
½ teaspoon sugar
⅛ teaspoon ginger powder
⅛ teaspoon cinnamon

Topping:
1 tablespoon gluten-free old fashioned oats*
½ tablespoon sugar
1 teaspoon gluten-free flour
⅛ teaspoon ginger powder
Pinch of salt
1 teaspoon oil

*NOTES
*Always check the ingredient label of the oats to ensure they are free of any allergens you avoid (see page six).

DIRECTIONS

To make the ginger pear filling:
IN A RAMEKIN, toss the pears in the sugar, ginger, and cinnamon, until fully coated.

To make the topping:
In another microwave-safe bowl, combine the oats, sugar, flour, ginger, and salt.
Stir in the oil.
Microwave the topping for 30 seconds (900 watts). Mix well, then microwave for an additional 30 seconds (900 watts).

Sprinkle the topping over the pears, and microwave for one minute (900 watts).
Let cool for two minutes, then enjoy!

Mango Matcha Tart

INGREDIENTS

Tart Shell:
1 tablespoon gluten-free flour
1 teaspoon sugar
¼ teaspoon matcha powder
Dash of salt
½ tablespoon butter (substitute a
    vegan buttery spread as needed)

Mango Filling:
1 teaspoon sugar
⅛ teaspoon matcha powder
⅓ cup chopped mangos

DIRECTIONS

To make the tart shell:
IN A RAMEKIN, mix the flour, sugar, matcha
powder, and salt. Mash in the butter with a
fork until the mixture is crumbly.
Flatten the dough into the bottom of the
ramekin using the back of a spoon.
Microwave for 15 seconds (900 watts).

To make the mango filling:
In a small bowl, mix the sugar and matcha
powder.
Pat the mangos dry with a towel.
Add the mangos to the bowl, and mix until
they are coated with the sugar and matcha.

Arrange the mango mixture on top of the tart
shell in the ramekin.
Microwave for 45 seconds (900 watts), then
let cool for two minutes.
Enjoy!

Cookies & Bars

Chocolate Chip Cookie

INGREDIENTS

2 ½ tablespoons gluten-free flour
2 tablespoons brown sugar
1 tablespoon nondairy milk
1 teaspoon oil
¼ teaspoon vanilla extract
Pinch of salt
1 tablespoon chocolate chips*

DIRECTIONS

IN A RAMEKIN, mix the flour, brown sugar, milk, oil, vanilla extract, and salt.
Stir in the chocolate chips.
Microwave for 45 seconds (900 watts).
Let cool for two minutes, then enjoy!

*NOTES
Always check the ingredient label of the chocolate chips to ensure they are free of any allergens you avoid (see page six).

Oatmeal Raisin Cookie

INGREDIENTS

3 tablespoons gluten-free old
   fashioned oats*
1 tablespoon gluten-free flour
¼ teaspoon cinnamon
⅛ teaspoon baking powder
1 ½ tablespoons brown sugar
1 tablespoon nondairy milk
1 teaspoon oil
1 tablespoon raisins

DIRECTIONS

IN A RAMEKIN, combine the oats, flour, cinnamon, and baking powder.
Mix in the brown sugar, milk, and oil, then stir in the raisins.
Microwave for 45 seconds (900 watts).
Let cool for two minutes, then enjoy!

*NOTES
Always check the ingredient label of the oats to ensure they are free of any allergens you avoid (see page six).

Double Chocolate Coffee Cookie

INGREDIENTS

2 tablespoons gluten-free flour
1 teaspoon unsweetened cocoa powder
¼ teaspoon instant coffee powder
Pinch of salt
1 tablespoon brown sugar
1 tablespoon nondairy milk
½ tablespoon oil
1 tablespoon chocolate chips*

DIRECTIONS

IN A RAMEKIN, combine the flour, cocoa powder, coffee powder, and salt.
Add the brown sugar, milk, and oil, and mix until fully combined.
Stir in the chocolate chips.
Microwave for 30 seconds (900 watts).
Let cool for two minutes, then enjoy!

*NOTES
Always check the ingredient label of the chocolate chips to ensure they are free of any allergens you avoid (see page six).

Spoonable Cookie Dough

INGREDIENTS

2 tablespoons gluten-free flour
1 tablespoon + 1 teaspoon brown sugar
2 teaspoons nondairy milk
½ teaspoon oil
Pinch of salt

*NOTES
Always check the ingredient label of the chocolate chips to ensure they are free of any allergens you avoid (see page six).
Wild blueberries are the perfect size for the lemon blueberry cookie dough.
Four servings of dough are pictured. The recipe can effectively be doubled, tripled, etc.

DIRECTIONS

IN A RAMEKIN, combine all the ingredients. Then, choose your flavor below!

Double Chocolate
Mix ½ teaspoon cocoa powder and 2 teaspoons mini chocolate chips* into the dough.

Lemon Blueberry
Mix ½ teaspoon lemon juice, ½ teaspoon lemon zest, and 1 tablespoon blueberries* into the dough.

Mint Chocolate Chip
Mix ⅛ teaspoon peppermint extract and 1 teaspoon mini chocolate chips* into the dough.

Snickerdoodle
Mix ½ teaspoon of cinnamon into the dough. Top with cinnamon sugar.

Ginger Molasses Cookie

INGREDIENTS

2 tablespoons gluten-free flour
¼ teaspoon cinnamon
⅛ teaspoon ground ginger
1 tablespoon brown sugar
2 teaspoons nondairy milk
1 teaspoon oil
½ teaspoon molasses

DIRECTIONS

IN A RAMEKIN, whisk together the flour, cinnamon, and ginger.
Add the brown sugar, milk, oil, and molasses, and mix until the dough is smooth.
Microwave for 45 seconds (900 watts).
Let cool for two minutes.
Enjoy!

Lemon Shortbread Cookie

INGREDIENTS

2 tablespoons sugar
1 tablespoon butter, room temperature
(substitute a vegan buttery spread as
needed)
1 teaspoon lemon juice
2 tablespoons gluten-free flour
Pinch of salt
Lemon zest, to taste

DIRECTIONS

IN A RAMEKIN, whisk together the sugar,
butter, and lemon juice until fluffy and fully
combined.
Mix in the flour and salt. Press the dough
evenly into the bottom of the ramekin.
Microwave for 30 seconds (900 watts).
Let cool for two minutes.
Top with lemon zest, then enjoy!

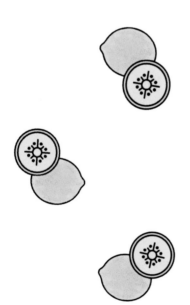

Dark Chocolate Brownie

INGREDIENTS

1 tablespoon gluten-free flour
1 tablespoon unsweetened cocoa powder
Pinch of salt
1 ½ tablespoons brown sugar
1 tablespoon + 1 teaspoon nondairy milk
2 teaspoons oil
1 tablespoon chocolate chips*

DIRECTIONS

IN A RAMEKIN, combine the flour, cocoa powder, and salt.
Add the brown sugar, milk, and oil, and mix to incorporate.
Stir in the chocolate chips.
Microwave for 45 seconds (900 watts).
Let the brownie cool for two minutes, then enjoy!

*NOTES
Always check the ingredient label of the chocolate chips to ensure they are free of any allergens you avoid (see page six).

Coconut Macaroon

INGREDIENTS

¼ cup + 2 tablespoons unsweetened
   shredded coconut
1 tablespoon honey
1 teaspoon coconut flour
Pinch of salt

DIRECTIONS

IN A RAMEKIN, combine the shredded
coconut, honey, coconut flour, and salt.
Microwave for one minute (900 watts).
Let cool for two minutes.
If you wish, drizzle extra honey and sprinkle
coconut on top of the macaroon.
Enjoy!

Deep Dish S'mores

INGREDIENTS

2 tablespoons + 1 tablespoon crumbled graham crackers* (separated)

2 tablespoons + 1 tablespoon mini marshmallows (separated)

1 tablespoon + ½ tablespoon mini chocolate chips* (separated)

DIRECTIONS

IN A RAMEKIN, add 2 tablespoons of graham crackers; then, layer 2 tablespoons of marshmallows. Top with 1 tablespoon of chocolate chips.

Layer an additional 1 tablespoon of graham crackers, 1 tablespoon of marshmallows, and ½ tablespoon of chocolate chips, in that order.

Microwave for 30 seconds (900 watts).

Enjoy immediately!*

*NOTES

Always check the ingredient label of the graham crackers and chocolate chips to ensure they are free of any allergens you avoid (see page six).

Make sure to enjoy your deep dish s'mores as soon as they are ready. They will harden quickly if refrigerated or left out!

Sweet and Salty Surprise Bar

INGREDIENTS

2 teaspoons honey
1 teaspoon oil
¼ teaspoon vanilla extract
½ tablespoon chocolate chips*

*Mix-Ins**
Cereal
Granola
Crushed pretzels
Potato chips
Cookie crumbs

DIRECTIONS

IN A RAMEKIN, mix together the honey, oil, and vanilla extract.

Add any ingredients of choice from your pantry. Cereal, granola, pretzels, chips, and cookies all make delicious additions.

Stir until all of the ingredients are fully coated with the honey mixture.

Mix in the chocolate chips.

Microwave for 30 seconds (900 watts).

Let cool for five minutes, or refrigerate to make a snack bar. Enjoy!

NOTES
Always check the ingredient label of the chocolate chips and all mix-ins to ensure these foods are free of any allergens you avoid (see page six).

Cinnamon Swirl Cereal Treat

INGREDIENTS

3 tablespoons mini marshmallows
½ teaspoon oil
¼ cup + 2 tablespoons rice cereal*
¼ teaspoon cinnamon
Cinnamon sugar, to taste

DIRECTIONS

IN A RAMEKIN, mix the marshmallows and oil. Microwave for 20 seconds (900 watts), or until the marshmallows begin to puff up. Quickly stir in the rice cereal and cinnamon. Continue to stir until the rice cereal is fully coated in the cinnamon and marshmallow mixture.

Top with cinnamon sugar, and let the treat sit for at least ten minutes. Enjoy!

*NOTES
Always check the ingredient label of the rice cereal to ensure it is free of any allergens you avoid (see page six).

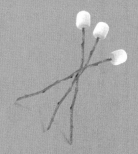

Notes

Use this space to write down your original ideas. Make note of favorite toppings, cooking time adjustments, ingredient substitutions, and more!

About the Author

Kristin is delighted to share her passion for baking through *Single Sweets*, her debut cookbook.

Diagnosed with celiac disease at six years old, Kristin is strictly gluten-free, and while baking, she also accommodates egg and dairy intolerances in her family. Kristin is a healthy living advocate who loves to try new allergen-free foods, whether homemade or from the store.

Kristin is currently 16 years old and a high school junior. In addition to spending time in the kitchen, she leads multiple clubs, many of which are related to science. She is also the co-founder of the nonprofit Care-Full, which delivers personal protective equipment to those in need during the COVID-19 pandemic.

Kristin lives with her parents, cat, and dog in Northern New Jersey.

Made in the USA
Monee, IL
20 January 2022